# INTRODUCTION

The memory is a fallible instrument and while we may think we know how our town has [...] when shown old photographs of the area, that our memories have led us astray. This bookl[...] of what Colwyn Bay looked like in the past and hopefully to stimulate an interest in the [...] that you may well be surprised anew by what you find in these pages.

In 1879, fourteen years before Colwyn Bay had a fire-engine and eight years after the local people tore down the toll gate at the end of Greenfield Road and flung it into the sea, Tennyson began his poem 'Old Ghosts' with the words: "Ye know that History is half-dream..." We make of our past what we wish and there are times when the Colwyn Bay of bygone days may seem to be something other than how it occurred at the time. We cover the past with our own individual brush strokes of memory. Perhaps these pictures will help you to realise the atmosphere and reality of those far off days.

A hundred and forty years ago, the bay of Cowlyn was occupied by a single substantial building, then the mansion of Lady Erskine, now the Rydal Preparatory School. In the span of a hundred years, the Colwyn Bay area has been transformed from a quiet farming backwater to a rather superior holiday resort and has progressed to to-day's bustling commercial centre. Two hundred years ago for the few people scattered in the area there was no idea of change or improvement in any form. They lived in their villages, Llandrillo, Llysfaen, Old Colwyn and when they died, everything was exactly the same as when they were born. In the years that have followed the look of the town has changed out of all recognition, but many of the original buildings still stand, (many with the dates of their erection on the facade), hidden among the ever growing number of new office blocks, shops and housing estates.

In the 1790s, our very first tourist arrived on the scene and was pleased with what he saw. Pennant with his band of horsemen arrived from Conwy at Rhos Point and wrote: "From Rhos Fynach the land recedes inwards, and forms a pretty bay. The country slopes to the water's edge, and is varied with woods and cultivation; Penmaenrhos, a great limestone rock, juts into the sea at the end of the bay." This view, in 1991, can still be seen in outline, but has now been more or less filled in by the habitation of mankind.

When Thomas Telford visited Colwyn Bay in 1811 and reported on our main road, then known as London Road, and suggested some improvements, it was still a place where most people walked everywhere. In 1844, the Parish of Colwyn was created, mostly out of Llandrillo parish. But it was only in September 1865, when Lady Erskine finally came to sell her home, Erskine House and her land, which included the Bodlondeb estate (1,850 acres) and the Pwllycrochan estate (1,191 acres), that Colwyn Bat started to emerge from an age reminiscent of feudalism to the more developed and urban times with which we are more familiar. So Colwyn Bay is essentially a relatively new town. Indeed, the railway did not reach Colwyn Bay until 1848, by which time, there were trains in India, South America and the United States of America. It was still a world of small horizons when, without television or newspapers, unreality began at the end of the high street. And an old lady, who when told that the price of candles had gone up because of the Spanish-American War, said: "Get along. Don't tell me they fight by candles ..."

Even in 1900, Rhos-on-Sea was still remote from Colwyn; the only way a vehicle could get there was via Conwy Road, Tan-y-Bryn Road, around Bryn Euryn, and then down Rhos Road. In 1915, the Rev J H Howard described Colwyn as a "garden with few weeds", and said that in those days the town was known as the "Garden City of the North". He wrote that from Penmaenhead, the town was "a semi-circular gem of beauty". In 1928, the *British Medical Directory* emphasised that Colwyn Bay was a "winter resort for aged and infirm persons and for delicate children." Its readers were told that the climate was rather dry for a westerly coast resort and said that "hydrangeas, yuccas and eucalyptus flourish out of doors." While a brochure printed for the Local Authority called *Health and Strength* said that the Colwyn Bay of 1928 was a "sure refuge of many who seek shelter from the ills of life, and has proved a kindly foster-mother, with health and strength in the fold of her garment."

I trust that the following pages will help to remind you of the days of greater tranquility, less urbanisation and of buildings long since forgotten. The pictures are set out, roughly following a route from Old Colwyn, through Colwyn Bay via the Abergele Road and Conwy Road, with detours to the promenade and side streets, via the West End of town and thence to Rhos-on-Sea, after a glimpse of Mochdre.

In compiling this history, I have been helped enormously by Alister Williams whose initial idea it was to put such a record together and to the Clwyd Library & Information Service and the Clwyd Record Office for allowing access to their unrivalled collection of pictures of Colwyn Bay; I am particularly indebted to Mrs Rona Aldrich, the Divisional Librarian and her staff at the Colwyn Bay Library. I am also grateful to the following people for allowing me to nibble away at their memories; Mrs Louisa Cheadle (100 years old and going strong), Ida Beardsall, Joe Davies, Amy Fairclough, Alice Firth, Evus Guard, Hugh and Margaret Holland and George Mellor; and finally I am grateful to my wife Constance, who insisted on correcting all my spelling mistakes.


Graham Roberts

Rhos-on-Sea, 1991




**Picture Credits**
Clwyd Library & Information Service: Front cover, inside front cover, 1, 2, 3, 4, 5, 7, 8, 9, 10, 11, 12, 13, 15, 16, 17, 18, 19, 21, 22, 25, 26, 27, 29, 30, 31, 32, 33, 34, 40, 41, 42, 43, 45, 46, 47, 52, 53, 54, 55, 56, 57, 58, 60, 61, 62, 63, 64, 66, 67, 68, 69, 70, 71, 72, 73, 74, 76, 77, 78, 79, 80, 81, 82, 84, 85 Clwyd Record Office: 23, 28, 38, 39, inside back cover Edgar (Pat) Allen: 24, 49, 50 Ida Beardsall: 75 Mr & Mrs Alun Davies: 51 Ralph Colwyn Foulkes: 59 Gladys Jones: 20 David Nicholas: 35, 37 George Mellor: 36, 64 Graham Roberts: 6, 44, 65 Anne Hughes: 14.

## 1. ABERGELE ROAD, OLD COLWYN, c. 1910

In 1925, the first building on the left housed the Westminster Bank, then came Masons the newsagents and then Mr H O Hughes who had a hat-selling business. Mr John Hughes, who lived opposite the bank (in the house with a horse standing outside it), was the Old Colwyn lamp-lighter who, on New Year's Eve, would go through the village ringing a large bell.

## 2. MINERS LANE, PENMAENRHOS, c. 1910

When Abergele Road, on the right, was widened, the houses on the right and the shops on the left, on the corner of Miners Lane, were demolished. Those on the left were Lingards General Store, another shop, the Miners Arms Pub and then slightly behind these (and not in the picture) was the original Bethel Welsh Chapel which was later demolished and replaced by the present building, designed by Mr Sidney Colwyn Foulkes. The first sermon ever preached in the village was delivered by the Rev Azariah Shadrach of Trefriw on 28 May, 1804 in a cottage called Bryn-y-Gwynt.

## 3. LLAWR PENTRE, OLD COLWYN, c. 1890

This view shows the oldest part of Old Colwyn, taken from the top of Llawr Pentre looking down towards Abergele Road and the sea. The local wheel-wright ran his business from one of the houses on the left of the picture. These have since been demolished and replaced by houses built along the river Colwyn.

## 4. PLOUGH TERRACE, OLD COLWYN, c. 1900

The white buildings (Plough Terrace) on the left of Abergele Road have been demolished and replaced by a bus shelter and steps leading up to the Red Cross Centre. Behind this terrace, in Rhos Place, Rose Hill, lived John Vaughan, the joiner and undertaker. It is said that as soon as his wife heard that there had been a death in the village, she would put the pot of pitch on the fire, ready to line the inside of the coffin.

## 5. STATION ROAD, OLD COLWYN, c. 1890

Station Road (foreground) showing Queens Road running up from the left. The large block of houses to the right is Endsleigh Terrace, on Endsleigh Road. The three large houses to the left are on Sefton Road. All the buildings in the picture are still standing but all the fields are now occupied by houses.

### 6. THE OLD COLWYN CO-OP, c. 1930

This building still stands on Abergele Road, opposite the Marine Hotel. This branch, the main Co-op store in Sea View Road and the Llandudno store operated a different policy to that found in the industrial areas of North Wales - their main customers were the local landladies who were loath to buy CWS goods, prefering brand-name products. The Co-op left these premises in the late 1960s and the Colwyn Bay Motor Cycle Co Ltd, is now managed from this address.

### 7. MIN-Y-DON, OLD COLWYN, 1928

The opening of the Bowling Park and recreation ground. Cllr Price Evans, JP, Chairman of the Parks Committee, leads off in the first game, 18 July 1928.

**8. OLD COLWYN STATION, c. 1900**

The Old Colwyn Station, which was located on Station Road at the bottom of the present Queens Road, was opened by the London and North Western Railway in April 1884. It was closed in 1952. The booking office was built at road level while the railway was built on an embankment above. The passengers had to use ramps to get from the booking office to the trains. In 1913, there was a proposal to widen the embankment from the Penmaenrhos Tunnel to Colwyn Bay (at a cost of £29,000) but the plans were put to one side for the duration of the First World War. After the war, it was decided that the cost could not be justified and the scheme was abandoned.

### 9. COLWYN BAY, c. 1890

This picture was taken from the summit of Bryn Euryn. The lane running to the left from the railway bridge (now demolished) is the line of the present Brompton Avenue. To the right of the bridge is Conway Road Junior School, originally known as the Council Boys School (Headmaster - Mr W E Davies) and the Council Girls School (Headmistress - Miss Grindley). The school was built in the countryside for the benefit of the children's health. All these fields are now covered by houses and the picture shows clearly the original limits of the town of Colwyn Bay.

### 10. INCORPORATION OF THE BOROUGH, 1934

This picture shows the Mayor, the Rt Hon Baron Colwyn, PC, DL, (formerly Mr Fred Smith) arriving for the presentation ceremony of the Charter of Incorporation on 20 September. The Lord Lieutenant of Denbighshire, Lt Col R W Williams-Wynn, is standing on the left of the picture. Many of the chidren in the Borough were presented with coins and a sapling was planted in Eirias Park (a few feet away from the present-day location of the public toilets) to commemorate the event.

## 11. THE PROMENADE, c. 1895

The view looking east towards Penmaenhead. It is from this stretch of promenade, built on the beach itself, that the pier now extends. It was the second section of the promenade to be constructed and included rubble taken from the foundation trench of St Paul's Church. The Belvedere Hotel, on East Parade, (now demolished) can be seen on the right.

## 12. THE PROMENADE, c. 1910

A view showing the second phase of development of the promenade showing the original, more decorative shelters, lamps and benches . The second building from the right was the 'Wireless College', an early type of Technical College, where the training fee was 30 guineas (£31.50) for twelve months. In 1925, the Principal was Mr Gordon S Whale.

## 13. COLWYN BAY TANK, 1920 - 37

This First World War tank was put on display outside the Council Offices on Coed Pella Road, as a tribute to the town's war dead. In the background, the Mission Church (known as the 'Tin Church') can be seen on the corner of Lansdowne Road. The tank arrived on 12 January 1920 and was sold for scrap in 1937, fetching £40-10s (£40.50). When it was dismantled, the mud from the trenches of Flanders fell from the inside.

## 14. HOME GUARD, 1943

No.1 Platoon, 'C' Company of the Denbighshire Home Guard, led by Major F L Broad, MBE (middle row, 7th from the right) photographed at Eirias Park in front of the boating pool, 16 May 1943. The old band-stand, now demolished, can be seen in the background. Major Broad served in the Boer War (1899-1903), in India (1903-10) and throughout the First World War when he was severely wounded. During the 1950s he owned a garage on Carlton Road, West End.

## 15. WOMEN'S JUNIOR AIR CORPS, c. 1941

The Women's Junior Air Corps was one of the lesser known units of the Second World War. This picture shows the Colwyn Bay Motor Driving and Maintenance Section with the Group Commandant, Mrs A Gordon Bennett, in the centre.

## 16. COLWYN BAY SPITFIRE, 1941

During the Second World War, a week was devoted to raising money to cover the cost of Spitfire fighters. The average cost of one was £5,000, which Colwyn Bay duly raised. This aircraft, No P8529, was built at the Vickers factory at Castle Bromwich and named *Borough of Colwyn Bay*. On 8 April, 1943, Sergeant R Berry was carrying out a local flying practice in this machine when it went into a sudden dive and crashed at Air Drie Main Farm, near Slammanan, Stirlingshire. Sgt Berry, attached to No. 58 Operational Training Unit, was killed in the accident.

**17. A JENKINSON & SONS, c. 1910**
This was the green-grocers located on the corner of Abergele Road and Rhiw Bank Avenue; a business which was still in existence in the 1960s. It is now North Wales Antiques

**18. J LLEWELYN JONES, CHEMIST, c. 1930**
Mr Jones, the proprietor of this business, had originally worked for Clay and Abraham "Chemists to the Queen" before opening his own shop. The business is no longer in existence but the property still remains at 74 Conwy Road, next door to the present Barclays Bank.

**19.  ABERGELE ROAD,  c. 1900**
This picture shows the junction of Rhiw Bank Avenue (see also picture No 17) with a parade making its way towards Eirias Park.  Just visible on the right in the distance, is 'Clock House' (the clock still survives) which was originally called 'Emlyn' and was the first building to be erected in the 1870s on this section of the road.  In the 1940s and 1950s, this was the terminus for the trams.

**20.  CAFE ROYAL, STATION ROAD, c. 1930**
This premises is now Mackays clothes shop.  The Premier Café was on the opposite side of the road. The 4th lady from the left, pouring tea, is Mrs Bob Jones and the 6th lady from the right, the very small lady at the centre table, won the costume prize at the National Eisteddfod.

THE OLD STATION

## 21. & 22. COLWYN BAY STATION

The station opened in 1849 and was originally known as 'Colwyn'. In 1845, Mr Adamson, a chemist, being uncertain where the station was to be built, bought a shop in Penrhyn Road (now Charnleys opticians) and one in Station Road (now Stead & Simpson). When the station was built, he sold the property in Penrhyn Road. In 1889, one of the first pupils at Rydal school described the station as "a primitive affair ...indifferently lighted by oil lamps". The site of the station was chosen in deference to Lady Erskine's wishes.

In 1904, the station was completely rebuilt and the line was quadrupled. The present station forecourt, booking office and other facilities were opened on 29 April 1982.

## 23. RAILWAY STATION STAFF, c. 1890

The first Station Master at Colwyn was Mr Benjamin Jones. There are thirty-five men in this photograph which makes an interesting comparison with the present staff which only numbers eight at any one time.

## 24. GOODS DEPOT, c. 1890

Two removal wagons belonging to Daniel Allen & Sons at the depot. The house on the left was the residence of the Station Master.

## 25. THE STRAND DRESS SHOP, c. 1935

This business is no longer in existence but the property remains at 15 Abergele Road as part of Ivy House and is now run as Diamonds Gift Shop, opposite St Paul's Church. On the opposite corner, where Woolworths is to-day, in 1900 there was Robert's Drapery Store. Mr Robert's son was involved in what was classed as Colwyn Bay's first tragedy when he shot his fiancé who lived in Greenfield Road.

## 26. TOMKINSON STATIONERS, c. 1920

This shop is still in existence in Penrhyn Road but now trades under the name of Sheldons (after a previous owner) and is owned by Mr and Mrs D Hough. It is still a stationery business and the present facade was erected in the year of our present Queen's Jubilee. The alley-way on the right runs behind the shops into Station Road. Next door, to the left, was at one time the premises of A J Fleet & Son, retailers of musical instruments, which boasted the existence of "practice rooms for Professors and Students".

## 27. FLAGSTAFF ESTATE, 1909

Dr Walter Whitehead, an eminent Manchester surgeon, bought the Flagstaff Estate in the 1880s and hosted the Bards of the National Eisteddfod of Wales for the Proclamation Ceremony of 1909. The Bardic Circle is still in place, surrounded by sea lions, panthers, parrots and eagles, for the Flagstaff Estate is now the home of the Welsh Mountain Zoo.

## 28. THE CONGO INSTITUTE, c.1900

The Rev William Hughes travelled to Africa and brought back a number of boys to be taught in what he called the Congo Training Institute, which he ran from Myrtle Villa on the corner of Rosemary Avenue and Nant-y-Glyn Road (now a Child Health Centre). He chose Colwyn Bay because it was a beautiful town, with a mild climate and people that were "pious and obliging". The aim of the Institute was to give the boys a Christian education with a craft apprenticeship after which they would return to the Congo as missionaries. Some of the boys died and were buried in Old Colwyn Cemetery. One headstone reads: "James Jackson Kuofi, aged 19, died 14th April 1909, son of James Kuofi of Cape Coast Castle, West Africa". The Institute finally closed in 1911 after an article exposing Rev Hughes appeared in the magazine John Bull. Rev Hughes died in the Conwy Workhouse in 1924.

THE PIERROTS AND PROMENADE COLWYN BAY

## 29. CATLIN'S THEATRE, c. 1910

Designed by Sidney Colwyn Foulkes before he had qualified as an architect, Catlin's Theatre was demolished before the Second World War and the site is now marked by the public toilets on the promenade, below the railway station. In 1940, Mr Catlin was found guilty of "permitting music not of a sacred or classical nature" to be played on a Sunday, namely comic songs including "When I'm Cleaning Windows" by visiting star George Formby on 1 September. The case was dismissed, with Catlin only paying costs, due to his previous good record.

## 30. VISIT OF HRH THE PRINCE OF WALES, 1923

HRH The Prince of Wales is seen inspecting troops and other personnel on the promenade on the site, below the embankment, where the band-stand used to be.

## 31. ODEON CINEMA, 1939

Opened in 1936, the Odeon had seating for 1700 people. The first film to be shown, at a gala premier, was *The Ghost Goes West* starring Robert Donat. The cinema was demolished in October 1987 and the site, on the corner of Conwy Road and Marine Road, is now occupied by the Swn-y-Môr flats.

## 32. ROAD SAFETY CAMPAIGN, 1949

This photograph, taken outside the Odeon on a Saturday morning, after the children's film show, was part of a road safety campaign to encourage children to use pedestrian crossings. Mr Thorpe (cinema manager) is standing second from the left. The children are [L-R]: 1st: Ken Hughes, 3rd: Gwenda Healey (now Highton), 10th: Shirley Westwell, 14th: Shirley Sprigg, 16th: Ronnie Syfleet, 17th: Peter Weston Hughes, 18th: Rosina Mellor (who now lives in Canada).

## 33. ARCADIA THEATRE, c. 1924

This building was designed by Sidney Colwyn Foulkes for Mr W Catlin for use as both a theatre and a cinema. In 1924, the resident manager was Wallace Kennedy. It was located next door to the Post Office on Princes Drive and was demolished in February 1981 to make way for the new A55 road.

## 34. COLWYN BAY CRICKET TEAM, 1947

Back row [L-R]:
C Paffey (scorer), J Lloyd (umpire), C Bennett, J Baggs, J Wooler, J Hardman, P Billinghurst.

Front row [L-R]:
Unknown, J Humphreys (Everton FC centre half during the 1950s), S W Newnham, R H Moore (Capt - ex Hampshire CCC where he was the first player to score 300 runs in one day), A Cassley, G Hodgkinson, E Lewis.

## 35. THE COLLEGE SCHOOL, c. 1938

These two buildings are now the Marine Hotel and the Toad Hall Pub and Restaurant on the promenade.

## 36. OLD COLLEGIANS, 1931

Back row [L-R]:
Unknown, unknown, Dick Butler, Eric Holt, Herbert Jones, Harry Butler, T Herber Davies (Headmaster & owner), Max Forbes, Gilbert Emery (motor cycle shop proprietor and TT rider), unknown, Geoff Earp, unknown.

Middle row [L-R]:
Ivor Hunt (chemist), unknown, unknown, Reg Bowes, S Rothwell, unknown.

Front row [L-R]:
Unknown, Ivor Davies, John Earp, unknown.

COACH AND
MOTOR TOURS

J. Fred. Francis
& Sons

Coach & Carriage Proprietors,
— COACH BUILDERS, —
Coal and Coke Merchants,

Tel. No. I. THE MEWS.

**37. THE MEWS COACHING POST, 1909**

A popular tourist attraction was the stage coach tours operated by J Fred Francis & Sons. Their premises were located next door to the Central Hotel in a building that has now been demolished. Note the interesting telephone number.

**38. CONWY ROAD, c. 1920**

A view looking west. On the right is the Central Hotel public house with the coaching office of J Fred Francis & Sons just beyond. On the left is the North & South Wales Bank (now the Midland Bank) whose name can still be seen affixed to the wall.

## 39. & 40. CONWY ROAD, c. 1900

A view looking west towards Rhos-on-Sea. Llewelyn Road is on the left, the building on the corner is now the premises of Lloyds Bank. The verandah on the right has gone and Barclays Bank now occupies the corner building on the right, opposite the English Presbyterian Church. Above Barclays used to be the Colwyn Bay Gentlemans Club. The town's first Fire Brigade was housed in a building (just out of the picture) in the left background. In 1881, a fire in Station Road was put out by neighbours despite blinding and suffocating smoke. One of the residents reported that, "A fire service is badly needed, although some individuals deny it isnecessary since the Llandudno fire engine, if telegraphed for, could arrive in about an hours time." (Llandudno is five miles away).

The lower photograph shows the same view in reverse. The building on the right was the Estate Office.

### 41. THE PIER KIOSKS, c. 1899

This photograph shows the pier kiosks being built. Beautifully designed and constructed they survived the two pier fires only to be demolished during the 1970s when the Golden Goose Amusement Arcade was built at the entrance to the pier.

### 42. THE VICTORIA PIER, c. 1900

The first pile of the pier was driven into the sea-bed on 1 June, 1899. The first Pier Pavillion which can be seen here, was burnt down in 1922. The popularity of the wheeled bathing huts can be judged by the large number on the shoreline.

### 43. THE VICTORIA PAVILION, c. 1910

This grand interior was totally destroyed when the pavilion burnt down in 1922 and its successor was a much less elaborate affair with a smaller stage and no balcony.

## 44. THE PIER PAVILION, 1927

The history of this, the second Pier Pavilion, was even shorter than that of the first. Opened on 23 July 1923, it was burnt down in 1933. There was a small theatre on the end of the pier called the Alfresco Pavilion which was operated by the McAllister Follies. It also burnt down in 1933 and was not replaced.

## 45. THE PIER, c. 1950

Undaunted by the two fires of 1922 and 1933, the local Council (who had been the owners since 1923) built a third pavilion on the pier before the Second World War. In 1968, the pier was sold to Entam Ltd, a subsidiary of Trust House Forte and in 1979, it was taken over by Parker Leisure Holdings. The lifeboat displayed in the foreground of this photo-graph was used to raise funds for the RNLI.

## 46. IVY HOUSE, c. 1890

Ivy House was Colwyn Bay's first stone house built in 1865 by the turnpike on what was then the London Road. It still stands today opposite St Paul's Church, Abergele Road. A flourishing grocery and bakery business was run from these premises and the owner grazed his cows on the land now occupied by the church. A pulley can be seen lifting a sack of flour up into the loft on the left of the photograph. The original owner, Thomas Hughes, came from Maenan, near Llanrwst and named the house after his home. One of the first Sunday Schools in Colwyn Bay, known as the Colwyn Bay Station School, was held here and every Monday evening prayers were said in the kitchen. This continued until 1871 when public services began to be held in the carpenter's shop in Ivy Street, behind this building, on a site which is now an Eletcrical sub-station.

## 47. CORONATION COMMITTEE, 1902

Back row [L-R]: Hon Sec Mr T H Morgan, Hon Sec Mr E T Davies, Hon Sec Mr J H Roberts, Cllr J Dicken (Chairman Amusements Committee).

Front row [L-R]: Hon Treas Mr R Hughes Jones, Rev W Hughes, FRGS (Chairman General Committee), Cllr W Davies, CC, BG (Chairman Tea Committee), Cllr R E Williams (Chairman Procession Committee).

## 48. CORONATION LIBRARY, 1905

Opened by the Rev Thomas Parry, JP, CC, on 24 April 1905, the public library was built to commemorate the coronation, three years earlier, of King Edward VII. The Scottish-American multi-millionaire, Andrew Carnegie contributed £3,800 towards the total cost of £5,436 (inclusive of the land and building costs).

## 49. & 50.  DANIEL ALLEN (1838-1904)

Daniel Allen was, with his wife Elizabeth, the founder in Leek, Staffordshire, in 1869, of the company Daniel Allen & Sons.  In 1883, they moved to Station Road, Colwyn Bay where the business became one of the most prestigious in the town, with a floor space of 20,000 square feet.  They sold furniture, china, carpets and also acted as funeral directors.  In the early days, the company held agencies for, and sold, all the best makes of pianos but, realising that this was not a part of the image that they wished to create, they released one of their staff, Mr Fleet, who then founded the piano and music shop in Penrhyn Road. In the late 1890s, there was a line of white posts along the middle of the pavement on each side of Station Road, marking the boundary between private and public property.  They were removed when the shopkeepers and the Council came to an agreement on the subject of verandahs and it was Daniel Allen & Sons that started the movement to improve the shops along Station Road.

The shop closed in October 1971 because the directors felt they could no longer find goods to sell which were of the fine quality their customers were used to.

## 51. STATION ROAD, c. 1890

The gateway which can be seen in the bottom left hand corner of this photograph led to the first Presbyterian Church to be established in Colwyn Bay - the Central Hotel now stands on the site. The shop on the right was demolished to make way for Wood's department store (now the Co-op), which was designed by Sidney Colwyn Foulkes. Further down the road on the right, was Daniel Allen & Sons' department store. Station Road was always considered to be the main shopping area of the town and the first Police Station was located there on the left hand side. The 1875 Ordnance Survey map of Colwyn Bay shows a cluster of houses and shops confined almost entirely within the triangle comprising the bottom right hand corner of the picture, along Conwy Road to the top corner of Sea View Road, where the Royal Hotel now stands, and then down Sea View Crescent to the bottom of Station Road.

## 52. D JONES & CO, CYCLE SHOP, 1899

This shop was built in 1896 on Sea View Road at the corner of Back Bay View Road, immediately behind the Union Church. It still stands today having been used by the Co-op from the 1940s to the 1960s and as a branch office of a national firm of funeral directors for one year in the 1980s. It has now been purchased by a Housing Association and is being converted into flats.

## 53. ABERGELE ROAD, c. 1900

This photograph shows the junction of Mostyn Road on the left. On the right is Oaklands (Amphlett's solicitors office), built in 1877 and still, 114 years later, one of the largest buildings in Colwyn Bay. Next door to the Oaklands is the old Town Hall, now demolished. Between these was the old Fire Station. The row of houses on the left are now all shops and offices, while in the background can be seen the English Presbyterian Church. Since this picture was taken, the building which now houses the Royal Bank of Scotland has been built between the houses and the church.

## 54. CATLIN'S PIERROTS, c. 1907

The Pierrots are seen here advertising a benefit performance for Sydney Freres, Mr Catlin's top comedian and singer. When Freres left Catlin's employment, he bought the Rhos-on-Sea Playhouse which is still situated on Penrhyn Avenue and is now used as a Co-op food store. This photograph shows the open air stage which was located on the promenade between the pier and the Colwyn Bay Hotel.

## 55. HARRY REYNOLD'S MINSTRELS, c. 1910

This stage was located on the promenade between the Pier and Eirias Park. George Elliot, a member of this minstrel company went on to become the famous 'Chocolate Coloured Coon'. The stage was eventually extended and had towers built on either side which were used as dressing rooms.

## 56. COLWYN BAY HOTEL, c. 1905

Once the sale of the Pwllycrochan Estate had taken place in 1865, little time was lost in the erection of this hotel. This stretch of the original promenade was known as 'The Parade'. In 1872, it was reported that "Mr Douglas of Chester furnished designs for the erection of a large and commodious building in every way suitable for the rising locality... a really splendid hotel rears its massive form in view of every traveller by the railway". The hotel was demolished in 1975 despite the pleas of John Betjeman who wrote to the press praising its architectural significance.

## 57. MARINE ROAD RAILWAY BRIDGE, c. 1908

This road was originally called the Sea Shore Road. A corner of the St Enoch's Hotel can be seen in the top left hand corner of the picture. The Colwyn Bay Hotel was located under the bridge and to the right. The A55 dual carriageway now runs across this area. The van was probably a removal wagon belonging to Daniel Allen & Sons.

## 58. AIR MARSHAL SIR DENIS CROWLEY-MILLING, KCB, CBE, DSO, DFC

Sir Denis was born in Rhyl but was brought up in Colwyn Bay (at Westbury, on the Promenade, and Carrington, Kings Road). A member of the RAFVR, he flew with 607 Squadron in the Battle of France and the Battle of Britain (destroying 4 enemy aircraft). In 1941, serving with 610 Squadron, he was shot down but evaded capture and returned to Britain via Spain. In 1942 he was given command of 181 Squadron flying Typhoons. At the end of the war he was credited with the destruction of 8 enemy aircraft). He took part in the first Battle of Britain fly-past and in the 1953 Coronation fly-past.

## 59. SIDNEY COLWYN FOULKES, 1885 - 1971

Sidney Foulkes was the foremost architect of Colwyn Bay. When he was baptised at St John's Church (which had been built by his father), the minister was insistant that he should have a second name and his mother chose Colwyn. He began his career by designing Catlin's Theatre and went on to design some of the most distinguished houses, shops, cinemas and churches in Colwyn Bay including the old Arcadia Theatre, Woods Department store, the War Memorials at Llandudno and Old Colwyn, most of the buildings in Rydal School, Old Colwyn United Reformed Church and the Council Estate on Elwy Road, Rhos-on-Ses. He was awarded the Freedom of the Borough in 1956 and was still working at the age of 85.

## 60. THE PROMENADE, COLWYN BAY, c. 1900

A view looking east showing, from left to right, The Colwyn Bay Hotel (built 1872), Balmoral flats (built 1892), the Majestic Hotel (built 1893), the Rothesay Hotel, Stafford House (which once housed Penrhos Girls School) and Westbury. With the exception of the Colwyn Bay Hotel, all these buildings have survived.

## 61. CONWY ROAD BRIDGE, c. 1890

This was originally known as the 'Board School Bridge' because of the close proximity of the local school (now called the Conwy Road Primary School) which stands behind the spot from where this photograph was taken. The houses in the background are on the present Rhos Road and Hermon Chapel now stands where the pine trees are in the picture. The bridge was widened in 1902 and eventually demolished during the 1980s when a new bridge was built over the new A55 road.

## 62. GLAN-Y-WERN FARM, MOCHDRE, c. 1930

All that remains of this farm today are the gate posts and entrance shown in this photograph; they can be seen opposite house No 309 Conwy Road, Mochdre. The farm buildings were demolished in the 1940s and, by 1951, the Borough Council had built 200 houses on the land, thereby doubling the population of Mochdre. Glan-y-Wern was a large farm which had, in 1846, according to the Assistant Tithe Commissioner for Llandrillo-yn-Rhos, a field called "Gadlas Felin Eithen", all trace of which has now vanished.

## 63. MOCHDRE MAY DAY PARADE, 1948

The annual May Day Parade started at the Mountain View Hotel, proceeded along Conwy Road, wound its way through the Council housing estate and finished on the football pitch behind J K Smits Factory. The 1948 Rose Queen was Barbara Jones of Wern Crescent and she was crowned by Marianne Davies of Mountain View. Barbara has now, in 1991, celebrated 30 years of marriage and has three sons and one grandchild. The farm cart was decorated with hundreds of paper roses by Barbara's parents and friends.

**64. RHOS COLLEGE, c. 1920**

Rhos College was built on the corner of Abbey Road and College Avenue by a Mr Glover as a school for boys aged eleven and upwards. Further down Abbey Road, at its junction with Marine Drive, was the area known as Rhos-Green Garden City. In 1922, one boy, Alan Roberts, was taken away from the Grammar School and sent to Rhos College because his father felt that at the Grammar School he was mixing with unruly boys like George Mellor. On the first day of term at the College, he met George Mellor who told him that he was there because his father had wanted him to get away from the 'rough' Alan Roberts!

**65. RHOS COLLEGE CRICKET TEAM, 1926**

Back row [L-R]: B Cameron, Aitken, C Hastewell, unknown, Bilton Langstaff (Headmaster).

Sitting [L-R]: S Edwards, R Harvey, Alan Roberts (Capt), Robson, George Mellor.

Front row [L-R]: Bourne, Roberts.

## 66. LLANDUDNO - COLWYN BAY TRAM, c. 1950

Work on the tramline was started in 1906 and it was originally a single line with passing places controlled by coloured lights and extended from West Shore, Llandudno to the tramsheds on what was then known as Tramway Avenue (now Penrhyn Avenue). In 1908 the line was extended to Colwyn Bay and, seven years later, to Old Colwyn. The Old Colwyn extension was cut back in 1930 and the trams were eventually replaced by buses in 1956. This photograph shows one of ten trams bought from Bournemouth in 1936. The company colours were green and cream and this particular tram is photographed in the Depot on Penrhyn Avenue, Rhos-on-Sea (the sheds are today used by the Lynx Express Delivery Service).

## 67. FIRST AEROPLANE TO LAND IN WALES, 1910

The actor, Robert Loraine, landed his Henri Farman biplane on Rhos-on-Sea Golf Course on 10 August 1910. Starting from Blackpool, he was attempting to become the first man to fly across the Irish Sea. After he had landed on the Golf Course trams were laid on to carry sightseers from the surrounding area. From here, he flew on to Anglesey where he was considerably delayed. Eventually, on 11 September, he landed in the sea, 100 yards off the Irish coast.

**68. & 69. RHOS PROMENADE, c. 1900**

The upper photograph shows, from left to right, No 8 Rhos Road (now Henry's Fish, Fruit & Veg Shop), Nos 77 and 79 Rhos Promenade (built in 1895), Welsh Calvinistic Methodist Chapel (now the site of Nino's Café), Dinerth House (now Flair and Browse Around), Penrhyn Avenue, Thorn Cotage, Horton Estate Office (demolished in the late 1940s) and 91 Rhos Promenade. It is thought that, at one time, a river flowed down Penrhyn Avenue joining the Afon Ganol which flows across the Golf Course.

The lower picture shows the view from the Cayley pub to the Rhos Abbey Hotel (just out of picture). This photograph, taken from the end of the pier gives a good view of Bryn Euryn.

## 70. BRYN EURYN QUARRY, c. 1895

The view looking west towards the Little Orme. The ivy covered chimney of Llys Euryn may just be seen in front and to the left of Llandrillo Church. The word Euryn is probably derived from 'aur' meaning golden or yellow hence Bryn Euryn would signify the golden or yellow hill, a reference to the appearance of the hill when the gorse is in bloom.

In the distance, the Vicars Road (now Llandudno Road) can be seen running across what is now Rhos-on-Sea Golf Course.

## 71. BRYN EURYN QUARRY & RHOS-ON-SEA, c. 1895

Bryn Euryn Quarry was developed in the 1840s. The photograph shows Bryn Euryn Farm and the line of Rhos Road down to the 'port' of Rhos.

**72. RHOS ROAD, RHOS-ON-SEA, c. 1890**

All the buildings seen here are still standing, with the exception of the one second from the left. When the road was widened, the cottage on the left (once G D Armitage & Co, solicitors) had its western end sheared away. This road is indicated on the map prepared for Robert Davies in 1763 and probably linked the Squire's home at Llys Euryn with the quay.

**73. RHOS-ON-SEA, c. 1900**

This photograph shows the coastline before the promenade was built. The large houses at top left are on Rhos Road. The buildings in the centre, at the point, which were built in 1865, were described at the time as "...a set of lodging-houses and a hotel, in which the spirit and letter of ugliness are carried out but too faithfully by an architect who, if his own handiwork be not the death of him, will surely live to see them pulled down as a nuisance." They are still standing!

## 74. RHOS-ON-SEA, c. 1901

The corner of Whitehall Road and the Cayley Promenade. The Mount Stewart Hotel now occupies the site above the earth bank on the left of the picture and the Aberhod Old Hall is in the trees in the centre.

## 75. BEARDSALL'S JEWELLERS SHOP, c. 1925

This shop is still in existence in Penrhyn Avenue. The Beardsall family arrived in Rhos from Manchester in 1915 and this was the last shop to be built before the outbreak of the First World War. Mr Eddie Beardsall (standing by the door) lived behind the shop where his mother took in vistors during the summer months. Edmund qualified as an optician in 1921 and the business is now carried on by his son Chris and his grandchildren Mark, Catherine and Johnathan.

## 76. RHOS FYNACH, c. 1930

Situated at Rhos Point next door to the Rhos Abbey Hotel, this house is one of the oldest in the district. The land was bought by Ednyfed Fychan in 1230 and the building was later handed over to the monks of Aberconwy, hence its name (Mynachdy is the Welsh for monastry). The house now stands untenanted and in a very decrepit state.

## 77. SINKING OF THE *RHOS NEIGER*, 1908

This photograph shows the wreck of the 196 ton *Rhos Neiger* which sank just west of Rhos Point; pieces of the vessel can still be seen at low tide. The ship had belonged to the Colwyn Bay and Liverpool Steamship Co before being sold to Captain Walter Hawthorn of Rhyl just one month before her final voyage. On 20 July she had collected 80 passengers from Llandudno and was about to pick up a further 75 from Rhos-on-Sea Pier for the return trip to Blackpool. Captain Smallman heard a "sudden grinding noise" from somewhere below the waterline as he ran the ship aground about 350 yards short of the pier. All the passengers were safely ferried ashore.

## 78. BLUE BELL HOTEL, c. 1900

By 1875, this public house replaced the Rising Gull (which is shown on a map dated 1763) at the bottom of Rhos Road. Located on the promenade, it is thought to have been called the Combermere Hotel at some stage of its existence. Today, the pub has changed its name yet again and is known as The Cayley Arms.

## 79. LLANDRILLO-YN-RHOS POST OFFICE, c. 1915

Built behind the Blue Bell Hotel on the promenade, this building is now a tea and craft shop called La Reina. It was a sub post office. The bay window on the left can be seen in the building behind the Blue Bell Hotel in picture No 77.

**80. THE PROMENADE, RHOS-ON-SEA, c. 1914**

The Rhos-on-Sea Pier can be seen in the background. The shops on the left are now faced with a verandah and the Neill's chemist shop now sells health foods. The trams used to pass this spot and then turn left into Penrhyn Avenue - the single track can be seen in the centre of the road with the electric wires, which provided the power, suspended from the ornate pillars on both sides of the road.

## 81. RHOS-ON-SEA PIER, c. 1912

This pier was erected in 1911, having been bought from the town of Douglas in the Isle of Man. During the Second World War, the Home Guard removed much of the wooden planking in the hope that any invading Germans would fall down the holes thus created. In March 1953, the Council decided, by two votes, to demolish the pier. The entrance area can still be seen at Rhos Point.

## 82. RHOS FYNACH WEIR, c. 1910

The foundations of this weir can still be seen on the sea shore just west of Rhos Point. At a Court of Inquiry held in 1867, it was stated that the weir, built by the monks of Rhos Fynach Monastry, had been in existence since the days of Magna Carta and could therefore continue to be used by its owner, Mr John L Parry-Evans with the proviso that a four-foot gap be made to permit the free passage of salmon. This picture clearly shows its value in terms of the quantity of fish caught.

**83. THE SHIP INN, LLANDRILLO-YN-RHOS, c. 1860**

This early photograph, although somewhat grainy in appearance, clearly shows the rural nature of the area around Llandrillo-yn-Rhos in the mid 19th century. The Ship Inn (centre foreground) was built by Robert Davies in 1736 and was demolished in 1874 and its name was later used by the present pub of the same name located in the field seen in this picture to the left of the road leading towards Colwyn Bay. The old vicarage, on the right, was built by the Rev Isaac Charles in 1762.

## 84. LLANDRILLO-YN-RHOS PARISH CHURCH, c. 1890

This church was originally the feudal chapel of Ednyfed Fychan, built in the 13th century, under licence from the Pope. When the old parish church disappeared in the submergence of the land now lying under the sea off Penrhyn Bay, Ednyfed handed over his chapel for the use of the parishoners of Dinerth. It has been enlarged over the years to its present size. It was constructed not only as a place of worship and sanctuary but also as a fortress in case of an enemy attack.

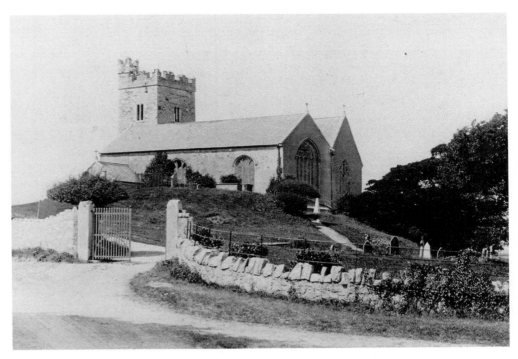

## 85. LLYS EURYN, c. 1890

The ruins of the old fortified manor-house built by the Conway family on the site of the palace of Ednyfed Fychan, 13th century seneschal to Prince Llywelyn the Great. This area is now totally surrounded by houses.

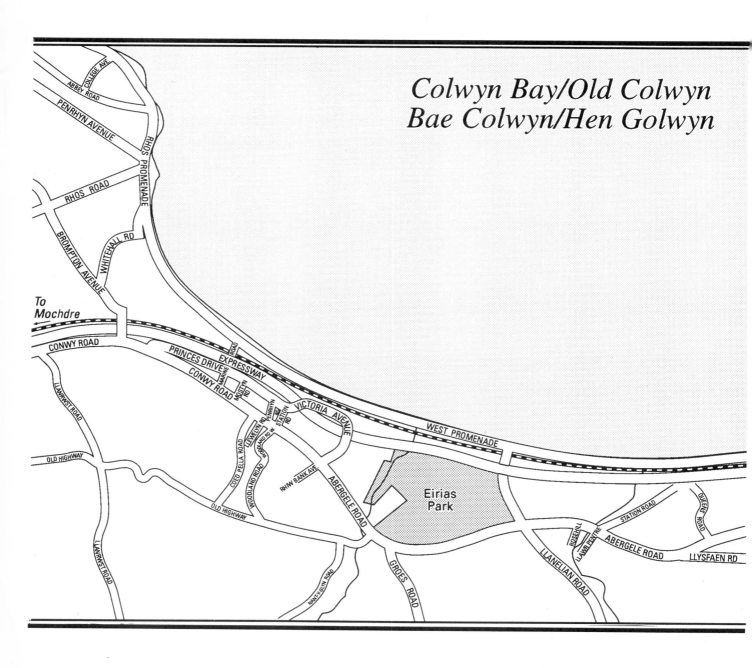

Colwyn Bay/Old Colwyn
Bae Colwyn/Hen Golwyn